The Horrible Warehouse

Of My Skull

A Collection of Dark Prose

Written by Michelle Brown
Illustrated by Michelle Brown and Roy Austin

To Roy and all the strong women in my world
Fiona, Caroline, and Lisa,
and all those who have supported me along the way.
For your unwavering belief in me I will be forever
grateful.

Eyes

The shiniest
of light filled specters
those spells of
your eyes
echoing
opportunities past,
new
possibilities
and
silent like
two natural
bodies
in my galaxy,
golden soaked
windows
poking out from
inside
you,
celestial
moons
I have carved
them a space
in my heart
where the dust of
this day
cannot touch.

Your face

The mess of my dress
sculptural
resembling
Rococo folds in your aftermath.
Rent by the olfactory dance of our scents
by the exquisite hues of you.

And the walls have creep onto our shadows
to penetrate your texture.
They too pine for your hard form
your magnetic touch in the cool night.
And I fall into that soft magic
of esoteric magnetism.

The simulacrum of our shapes
dancing in obscure universes
lurid in dark radiance
on the cold wall,
are still not as beautiful,
as your face in the shadows.

Alone 1

Oh, how I'd have loved to lay you there,
with your moist eyes and velvet hair,
skin softly glistening and the music I listen to.
Dim lights carelessly rearranging themselves
through my window.
But I was there in solitude,
alone with the dying scent of you.

I will wait awhile for this dose to seize me
until my body doesn't seem to
recognize me,
but right now
I'm comfortably numb
In my mad mind.
So I'll wait awhile
wait……..

until the universe embraces me
until the world has finished with me,
as my consciousness becomes infinite
and spreads out, despondent……

to my cold, corporal matter over there.
I'll wait it out in this terrifyingly beautiful
caravan of nowhere.

Singing odes to my cold god,
sweating over there
I'll watch him shiver
with my knees apart
I hope to touch his ashen, stony heart,
and wish to fuck that he would start,
to love me
to love my cold and selfish heart.

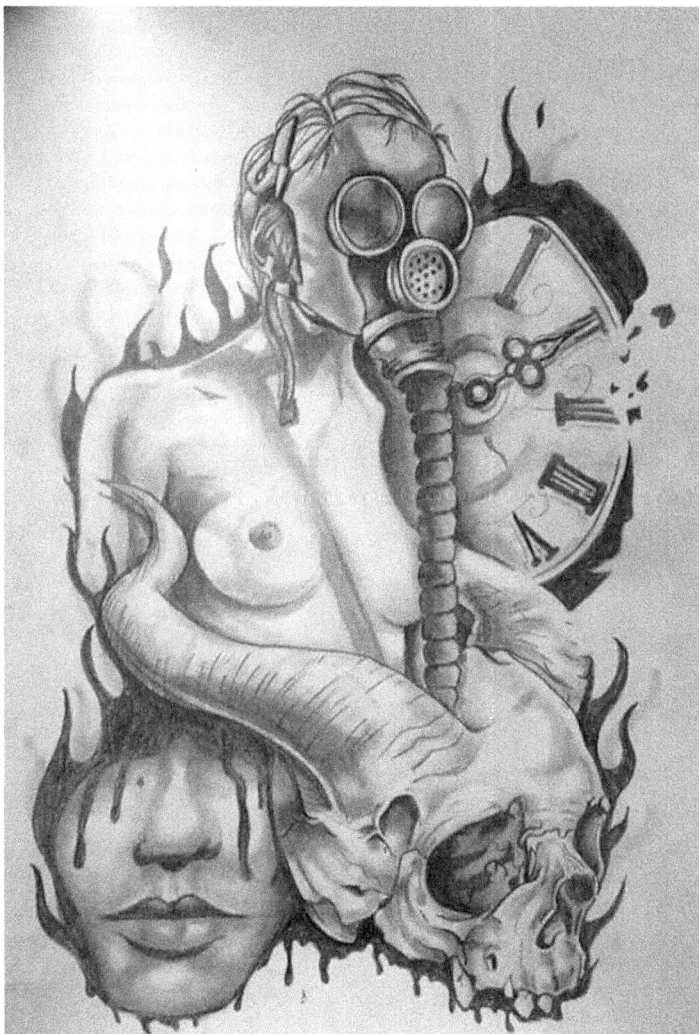

Our celestial lips dance

in a strange symbiotic mess
of ecstasy and movement
I chase the lonely seas of your eyes
and stand steadfast
to escape my stumbling into you,

I can dimly feel the warmth of my heart
From the sun that lives inside you
And my long, long, lateral longing
Of you, you who picks out stars for me
from every separate galaxy
And sends them to me in my dreams
You of impossibly beautiful smiles.

I dreamt of you

I dreamt of the unimaginably beautiful
scent of you on my skin,
as we'd lay clinging
in the night's purple formlessness.

I trailed your name lazily across my palm
with my cold finger, my invisible ink
burned somberly in your absence.

I traced the contours of your face in my mind,
the tactile qualities as I lay sleeping,
or at least how I thought they'd be.

I dreamt that I knew you,
knew you through shared memories,
how our entwined shadows
Would rise and fall and stain the wall.

I believed that we shared one another's clairvoyance
that you could be transported to me seamlessly
and that your words would never leave me
as I pined for your magic arms in the cool night.

The green night

Let my form
echo yours
so wonderful things happen
in that gibbousness moonlight
of hope and sound and light.

Press your palm against
my back and my waist
so that my steps quicken
towards you.

I'll have a delicious smile
that resonates
deep within
the core of you.

Our feet will
communicate a profound
longing, and the air
will have never felt
you quiver like this
and you'll whisper
really, really?
until my whole body aches.

In that phosphorescent
ecstasy of wills
let my fingertips trace
a silent stairway
to the euphonic
genius of you

whilst I in my verdant hue
beckon,
our crepuscular
figures awash
in the silent lament
of the moon.

Oh green, in the night
in that soft light
and I'll know I've
never been in this
quiet kingdom
except when my dreams
lullaby me.

We snuck like alley cats
through the mess that daggers make
and through all those magical dreams we made
I do hope death claims me,
with his universal tears.

11

Bid me good day, as the last shades of hue
leave your solitary form
on this grey day
and the hours seem to last a lifetime
as the cold air feeds of my abyss of lonesomeness
and the tears have never felt me quite like this.

Cold monsters return to me,
as I gaze despondently
through the dirt stained disconnect,
of my fast returning memories.

Chilling and wanton and mad
in the wilderness
your mad mind
carved up strange images of worship
then transported them to me
seamlessly through your clairvoyance
and eccentricity.
It's only you who disappears
through half lit caverns in my universe
emerging only to become subversive
and making me fawn at you
while I'm craving your residue.

Cold words

Only those who walk through fire
understand the loss of self
sleeping through the dour dew,
and sliding across those almond shaped eyes
and radiating arcs in the tar dark center of me.

I wasn't sure of myself
with prose and dead eyes
grave and grey, brown
listless as the last remnants of childhood
scrapped along my spine
injuring my heart,

recalling words shredding
with razor sharp precision
making every atom in my skin ache
to remind me of their own emptiness.

Tired

Walking on egg shells
for so many years
made my feet ache when flat
and always search for obstruction.

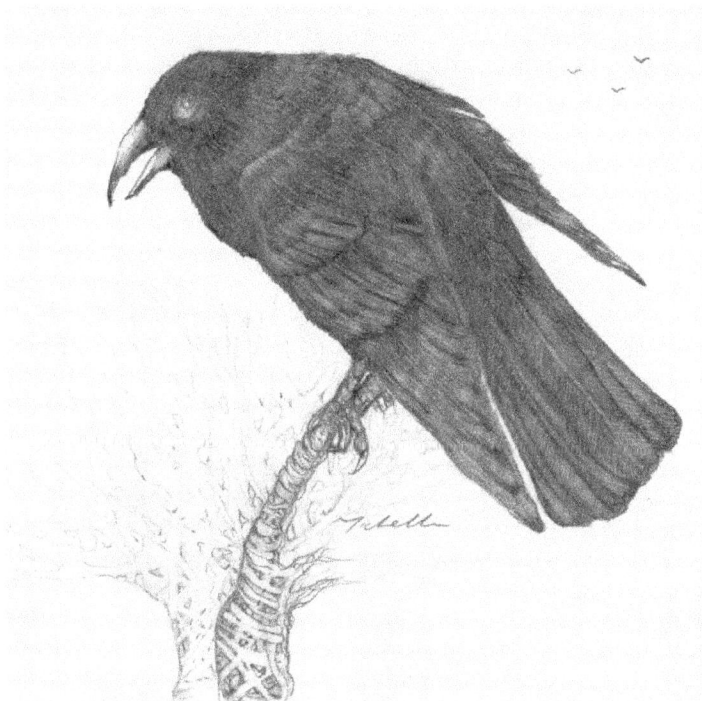

19

You're such a stunning display of innocence,
you're contrary to states of my soul,
injured and desperate, confused and messy,
the most perfect version of me.

Sunless

You with the endless love of smoke and mirrors
and machinery of flesh,
ploughed down on the long streets
of shadows, reprisals
I watched upon you,
your eyes too dead for dreams
glazed over, like some sickly, sweet
contortion of sugar.
I lived here so long with you
in this grey house
seared by dust
marred in the cold wake of my happiness
and no sun ever shone long enough to
remind me I was once alive…

The Clearing

Your flesh caresses me
firmly as we pace onward,
your dark eyes
top full with reason
watch the shadows dance
across our paths
while my lips pronounce your name
in many secret, long dead languages
as you drag me onward.
Your face is a poem
alive with thoughts,
my heart was a vault
that housed all my secrets,
but now
something terrifying inside me
lays wake in this soft light.
Your fingers clutched around mine
mirrors my wanton yearning
as our earnest steps quicken
we are almost at that clearing.

Blooming

It is only because I was
selfish and unassured
that tumours had blossomed
budded and bloomed
and burst forth
from deep within this tar dark heart of mine,
so now I am numb beside you
for you have told me that I am beautiful
and stared into my eyes
from another fixture in time.

Shocked out of the final remnants of sleep

Shocked out of that electrified journey
my dreams collapsed
and I emerged bleary eyed
into the karmic bombs
that have aroused me,
stumbling out from the madhouse of my soul
without wings
from an abyss of fins
and segmented eyes
awake from a coma of mad sea visions.
In my dreams you walked across the sands
dripping uncertainty,
pushing down imaginary walls
because I had abandoned you in heaven with your
post-human Jesus
you wore decorations of seaweed and light,
your mind was naked and beautiful and shone
with a wisdom beyond the heartbreak of creation.

A journey

He imagines different cars,
the skin trembles;
he rides with Virgil and Dante,
as he hallucinates his metal gods,
their hysterical screeching
in a chorus of hotrod angels,
as he drives across the supernatural darkness
to my door.

The break up

We once shone in the stale sunshine,
free-forming rain,
our last caress was a series of velvet moments
in a winter of discontent
as we traced the epiphany of night through
endless
depictions
of emptiness us...

Without sharing illicit rainbows of touch,
we the uncomfortable, apathetic furniture
longed for a deep otherness,
where sweet words would one day bloom
like soft, tumours on our lips as we celebrated new
forms.

My Passion

I see myself jumping or falling
into unfathomable depths,
we threw stones from my perch
where I had come to sit alone;
maybe someday my passion
that is so endless, dramatic and repressed
will open it's horrible dripping jaws
and finally run with it!!

Thinking

So I think of you in obsessed silence,
as I skim thin books about simplistic people
and take solace in my own pages of longing.

You

So numbed by your lovely physics
I forgot half of what you said
yet too strung out on your magic eyes
to be counted with the dead.

Us

Just us, sharing the same dream
in some near grubby ecstasy
in the horrible warehouse of my skull
in its preternatural sea.

The supermarket incident and other calamities

I saw myself mindless, lonely,
strung out on neon images,
shopping for a cure to my self-consciousness
in some Pentecostal church of you....

I saw myself in supermarkets aisles mouthing terrible
imaginings,
as I fingered the pumpkins, tore apart loaves of bread
and asked crazier upon crazier questions,
while shopkeepers and babies waiting to be born
spasm,
as I announced your enunciation.

My Christ-lust in this advertisement, emptiness,
your apathetic genius, the nothingness,
selling you, your brand name existential bullshit;

let's leave here now and journey on some superseded
pain,
some second rate longing in your god hotel;

and if you still can't feel... Then Jesus... just at least learn
how to touch.

A nice day in the matrix of your heart,
the sun kissing my skin gently as though whispering a
final goodbye in an overwhelming all pervasive sense of
stillness;
the beautiful gardens of you shone in several
arrangements of happiness
and in small invisible gestures of kindness.

Day two... observations

My skin sweats out evidence of chemicals and alcohol,
a chemist's array of solutions that never seem to solve
my problems.

Its thin condensation clings like ugly reminders of the
warm weather in this our uncomfortable greeting.

Empty beings lacking the ability to see beyond the latest
shiny thing,
caress me fiercely with their eyes,
I offer them nothing but a seeming warm, safe, blanket
of contentment
and the soft cadence of my sighs as I scream
hysterically across the dreamscapes of my mind,
with ugly unanswered riddles pouring from the
unfathomable darkness of my soul.

They smile blankly in return.

Visions of you

Cum encrusted visions
of wet versions of you
in a world of your body
that I want to intrude;
I feel my calm air is a thin veil
that I'm going to lose.

Because my yearning is palpable
in that dark cauldron of us
in the warehouse of my skull
of deviations and dust
and my numb body beside you
is a tower of dark, delight at dusk
with my hideous enlightenment
and my heart full of rust.

I am a soft instrument
For attracting your gaze
and I want you to want me
in so many horrible ways,
and I can't slow these awful images
that crown my palpable daze.

Play games

Play games with my crazed,
amazed mind,
with my spirit eyes,
my cumulative, cum encrusted, lust mantras
and be my lovely silver, gilled crustacean.

How I longed for your soft fins.

I show my amazing gratitude by leaving you gift
wrapped,
tinsel coated, sex crimes, in abandoned streets and
parks.

Wake me from my usual ecstasy by saying yes to my
throbbing gills and sudden movements in the soft,
murky light.

Yes to my scaly, cashew, shaped kiss
humming with weird sub-audible deviations.

We radiate in seven different colours
in several blue dimensions
without any hot dissension.

Lust mantras, perversely wonderful,
dripping tendrils of lovely us
giddy from the hot sun
shining in the wet garbage
existing in our own impossibly beautiful realm.

Kind eyes

I stole glances of you
in brief encounters
and I felt you were my familiar spirit
because the dead came to me
in my dreams more than dreams,
their drifting spiritual forms in the wet sunshine
and the concrete reality of me
longing for the deep otherness of you
explored through the rough love of
our lips chapped with miracles
long for the long beautiful sanctuary
of the pools
of your eyes, as deep as time
in secret golden, hazel worlds.

Free

All my ideas
fall from my mouth;
I'm announcing the truth,
singing it proud;
all the disorder,
the cold apathy,
I left it alone
and my visions are free.

If words are the tonic
for a beautiful life,
I'll wed those cold monsters
I'll be their good wife
and I'll stand alone
in a world by myself
but I will not be lonely
with all the books on my shelf.

Forget

Plastic discarnate entities in the dirt
stained disconnect of the machinery of reality;
are these masses always wrong?
forget them!

Wet promises, apt, leisurely feline cries
dreamscapes of your hands and eyes,
there's softness in forgetting
the lithe demonic figures in
the brine or the windswept, mindset
at the edge of reason or time.

Soft undulating forms line the water's edge
with small invisible, kind gestures
hedging bets
about us, call the hideous kinky windows of my mind
'A familiar reality' with your mouth or mind.

44

I sense the majestic truth of you;
for you placed strange fruit on my lips in my dreams
where our skins are connected through silence
and other intangible things,

and you made the harsh sun go away,
and with all your imagined flaws
to me you are perfect.

With segmented eyes
devious designs and neon glow dripping from my gaze
wet and amazed....
strung out on crazy visions of you searching for a
fevered fix.

Our conjoined memories of this blue hotel were
carmine coloured;
recall the mess of us made worse with razors,
god awful clothing and your utter lack of discomfort.

You saved me

You are the most perfect version of me,
because the world has collapsed leaving in its wake
a murder of tiny skeletal insects,
because we share ramshackle visions
and our mantras reach lithe,
discarnate beings with angel symmetry
and blighted, sexless power.

My mind is an archaic design,
a detached carnival,
an androgens Venus,
a euphemism for the collective us,
you saved me from my ramshackle arts
my pulpit of pain, my plasticity word porn
and all my horrible parts.

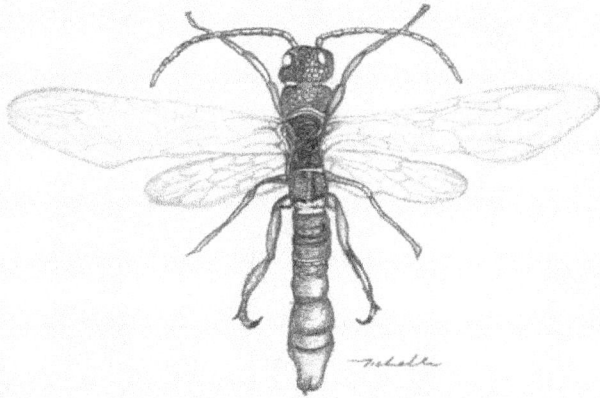

Memories

Pressed flowers in grey ripples,
the subdued light, reckless endeavours,
the restlessness of a past life,
graffiti, pigeons sleep inside dead trees,
while in confined spaces
our huddled figures connect with locked fingers.

We embraced in drains on overcast days,
walked on railway tracks at night
made genius art and beat poetry,
and I shot you up with anti-pain, fed you noodles,
dressed you in garbage bags and lipstick,
whilst mothering you senseless with sexual undertones.

I dreamt we retracted into the background;
our colourful natures
made great wall flowers
and we swayed
as the music played
the euphonic genesis of us
in the killing floor of the living room.

I think about you in dreamscapes,
in the violence of the perfumed night,
the speckled land in the aspect of your eyes
I have gazed upon your smiling face
as bright as a carnival,
the perennial beauty of your soul.

And if you were mine I'd love you as you grew old,
and know your body as I know mine,
until my last breath rejoins the heathen sky,
until we commune with the soil once more.

The wind was soft and dissident
and upon my solitary frame it crept,
and formed arcs around my heady breath
and spoke to me once more;
She spoke a silent litany,
for her lost love the deep blue sea,
and told me of all the things I'd find
if I let flowers bloom upon my lips
and gardens fruit inside my mind.

If You,

If you tell me you like the darkness
I will carve your name into my mind with invisible ink
Paint your name in wet circuses of light on my mirror
And my breath will labour under the spirits of my lips
While searching your eyes full of prose and certainty
I will compare you to the mountains
Those omnipresent giants, who have known the sun
and moon
And all the secrets of the moths,
Now I too will tell them your name
I'll write about you with my delicate visions
Compare you to the moon while I kiss away the dust of
the day
Through light soaked rooms
If you like the darkness
I'll drink in the sonnet of the woods
And liken you to the breath of Pan
I'll kiss the lines around your eyes
And recite words to you into the lull of your back
With my figure pressed firmly against you
Until your snores decorate the cool air
I'd be intoxicated by your touch
But still let you leave every day
A tourniquet of need
I'd write about you
We could be become soliloquies
Art personified
We'd be the loveliest words
And the most horrible,
The simplest words
The saddest structures on paper

Tangled hearts and veins in singular letters
I'd be pleading for your love in strangled remarks
Broken sentences
Burnt stanzas
I'd write you poetry
I'd furbish the walls of my empty soul
With my trembling want
If you like the dark
I would decorate your name with inky scars
On my lips and arms
As I offer you my heart.

These thoughts

These thoughts... consume me...
decorate me ...
Saturate my skin in pearls of sweat as I sway
uncomfortably in the dank theater of my skull
These thoughts cover me...
like blankets of shame, useless and full of holes and
mites as I struggle all night though terrible irritated
sleeplessness
These thoughts...
elevate me, present me to brilliant winged monsters,
light spilling through their deep set orbs, like nighttime
carnivals in an oasis
These thoughts present me with victory marches
through wormy rabbit holes
These thoughts. ..
Bite me ...with their snarling gnarled jowls…
Those rabid curled-up, tar-black lips, that tear me
asunder
under moons of hopelessness...
....and their mortuary cold steel eyes stare headlong
into my grey nowhere soul, as I stitch my wounds
together through the vicious sunlit day
These thoughts embrace me, completely...
like I'm the only warmth left in this mad collapsing void
And these thoughts....without a smile, nor word,
or touch
abandon me...

My delicious smile

I have a delicious smile
That resonates from deep within
that arcs magic and gold
and I rest my eyelids;
in the shimmer of shellac
you sow moths into my heart
they lay small, ecstatic eggs
and make me feel again,
and you tell me that I'm beautiful
with my explosive tumours
that bloom from deep within
my cherry scented lips,
are now always turned towards the sun
as I'm released from my cold tomb
with your warm hands.

Awake

I am now awake,
and shadows have crept onto our faces
in the collective morn,
and the moonlight has finished with her magic arms
in her soft eternity of stillness.

Your face is a sonnet of empathy
in the aftermath of the luxurious,
purple glove of night,
the time of my rescue.

And now our smiles are powerful and bright
like the soft, subdued,
sunlit cavities of our eyes,
and the hours have sifted by,
carrying the morning to us in diffused waves,
highlighting our now warm forms,
over brimming with a numb contentment.

I now know that night and day are full of goodness.

Were you my tower of hope
all along in that wet nothingness?

Did you disguise your lips
as those incandescent fleeting boats that have finally led
me home?

I've learnt that it's better to give and risk everything
and have it washed away
than to live in a minimal dream.

It's far better to live a brief moment in your smile
than float forever
in the purgatory of the placid and seductive void.

Smiling in circular madness

I have cylindrical smiles that burn with the desire of my
whole singular being.

And I want to breathe fire in the wet commotion of
your eyes
and tear those visions down,
and run with the scream of the world.

I show you my virtues with my rusty love
and though the miracles on our lips.

Visit you in miraculous rituals of touch
with the final mess of your skin
in a beauty personified
by the tired suffering of this world
made anew by the realms of our senses.

By the water

There we lay, beautiful in the grey overtures
of that strange landscape,
with the echo of a barely audible song.

We were snug in wet blankets of amazement
with only our tangle of limbs and seaweed
to starve of an audience of aquatic monsters.

They were shining,
standing strangely tall and defiant by the bank,
whilst I lay in the nape of your neck cooing
and expressing my concerns
through aqueous, cerebral imagery.

Fish shone at our feet in the wet sunshine of the water,
silver and real.
Their whole live, bodies flapping in and out
of their sunlit caves in their own preternatural voids.

The taller sea creatures soon grew tired of us
and joined the smaller fish,
marching headstrong
into their mess of movement and fins.

You were absently caressing the crook of my arm
and whispering over and over
"it's all going to be okay."

I believed you.
As we stared into the void with our hearts on our
sleeves and the love of the sea on our minds.

Silence

I bruised my mouth on my words
and was struck by a silence
deeper than your understated Orwellian worlds...

deeper than the vast oceans of your eyes

deeper than your legends

deeper than my repressed rage

where even the cicadas pause in their stunned
amazement.

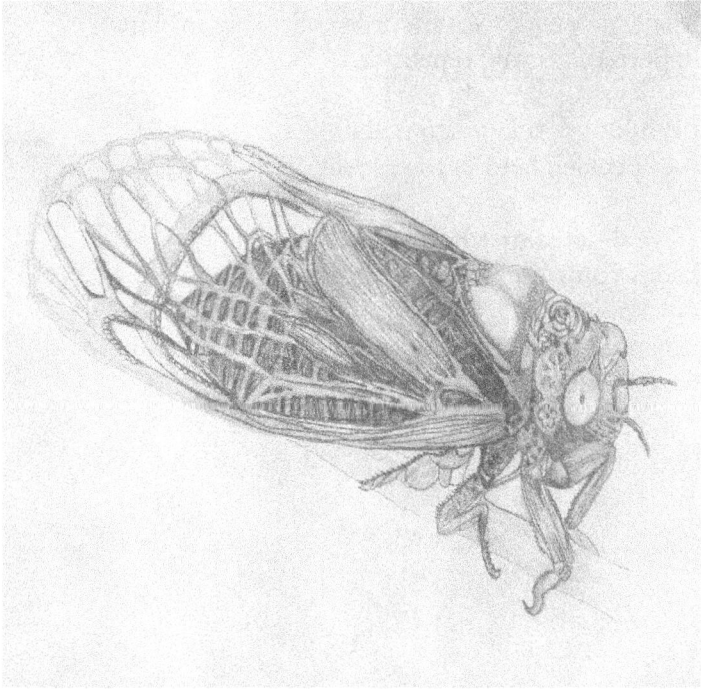

Will you be my guest of honour
and hold me with your gaze?

I have visions of your words collapsing into mine
in perfect, karmic repetition.

I think of you in perfumed nights,
the speckled land in the aspect of your eyes.

If we'd never met I'd have dreamt you up,
and if you were mine I'd know your body
as I know mine,
because I have carved you out of the sandstones and
deserts and clay monuments of my mind.

The scent of your wrist
bent doubled with mine
echoing the rent universe
of our lithe formless passion
see you, your waves of diffused sunlight
in the lazy afternoon of beautiful us.

I feast on no new figures.
my listlessness not wistful,
no new nightmares,
nor shadows in the shallows.

Just my sallow form
Pining over your grave,
grey lit glimmer
and my formlessness in your life.

In my visions our symbiotic, figures articulate a latent
urgency,
their soft forms make interesting patterns,
which melt into the formlessness,
the velvet recesses of night...

And I view you how you are now,
how I dreamt you up in the purple glow...
Did I also have similar features in your dreams?
I always see you as the most perfect version of me...

And our clairvoyance is everywhere
it's visual discrepancy palpable,
communicating with the air,
clad in weak, kinetic, creative energies
beautifying our visions...

Making our paths cross, making me remember you....

Beings far more beautiful than us live in the sea
I'm with them in my dreams
dreams of sand and substance
and tactile visions where I meet you.

Yeah! I want to
wrap myself completely in these shorelines of your eyes
sun drawing into the soft dusk cavities like ghost lamp
lit glowing embers in the dying day;
yeah I'd like to be destroyed
by those half lit parables gazing off into the far distance
stumbling into a truth and depth unreadable shining
beautiful in amber green waves being pulled
completely under
with my running thoughts of turbulence
and longing for oblivion.

Words

Citing enigmatic, ephemeral ink, sprayed in
preternatural arrangements
through the sultry air of our kiss, in invisible allegories
and spells of epitaphs and spittle,

Join me,
whisper words colder and further than the distance in
my eyes,
about as far as I'm prepared to go on this dark eve,
Past your beautiful injury of touch and the soft throaty
laughter of morning,

Simulate me with conversation through the copulation
of wet driven evenings,
the long lateral longing in habitual winter,
with your cryptic spirit eyes,
just past the cold summer of us
in amazing forms of sexual magic and singular
ideologies,
by being a creature with words stranger than my grimy
nefarious memories.

Day by day by day by day

Constriction, open cerebral, wounds in mandela worlds,
in the tar ravaged streets wet visions reigned,
without amazement or intricate designs,
we weaved no strange instruments of touch
with our half dead figures and automatic writhing,
writing, instructive, delusion in plasticity.

Carnivals of movements or confusion
seeking weak infusions of infinite dreams
to placate my increasing lust in the wilderness,
to forget you,
your instruments of pain.

My endless depictions of emptiness us,
and this banal reality once again.....

The magnificence of the night closes in
as we waft through her steely darkness;
I want to know you
trail curtains of night into your soft dawn
reveal the enigmatic genesis of you
through the ferocity of our lips
our clairvoyance is conductive
with the mess of our forms made art
in the violence of our warmth
my gorged out reanimated features shine
with the dead of my eyes telling no tales
except that I was once kind and talented.

Brandish flecks of golden ash
that rest upon my eyelids of lead
your touch quickens my cold flesh
in this wet darkness
and the carnival of our smiles
closes in;

We mouthed obscene words
and acts
in our minds
your dewy eyes
in this wilderness of night
searching for our lost moments
you cling to me
like a crazy hobo
with eschatological clairvoyance;

Your form fills my disjointed gaze
so rest kisses on my forehead
secure them there with golden ash
you tell me that my words stop your heart
like bouquets of bottle tops
and convulsive aneurysms;

the mess of my flesh is electric
with ash and gold
and your magnetic eyes
caressing my eyelids ajar
as we breathe in tiny monsters,
our collective amoebas
are euphemisms for the

collective us,

burnished hued
bush fire victims
are
mountains of us
in that furnace of our world.

Wake up

There's magic in the overcast morn,
I close my eyes, see the constant answers,
the endlessness of explanations,
the hideousness of knowledge
and the possibility of machinery,
all unintelligible to the humanity,
though I have come to know the universe
through their lack of significance;

They're all empty of meaning,
gratification,
or deep, spiritual understanding;
I clutch your rotting flowers in infinitum truth,
yet sense the lucid finality of it all,
hand in hand with epiphany day,
I rest forever in her warm hamlet
lacking, dour amazement.

Wake up! wake up!
Let images repeat themselves
and return to the ground,
I'm a hulled artefact with no internal life,
I have sensed the future
with the internal monologue of a bag lady,
the finality of it all.

I am balanced in a temporal void
like a corpse filled
with the drifting uncertainty of the tide.

Vibrating in and out of the same universe
tempting old forms of us
in the diffused light of sepia hued
kitchens amongst the wallpapers, paint,
dilapidated posters
and photos those old genuine smiles
once stood

metaphysical us,
feel your disingenuousness
through our collapsing hands, stolen glances
cold words.

Let's meet!

Let's meet
in the endlessness of this wet pursuit,
me erect like bayonet, baguettes
or bent languid,
clutching, cumulative, cum encrusted jewels of you,
while mouthing horrible imaginings.

These boots will take me anywhere,
so let's meet in some seedy hotel at the edge of hell,
decorated only by the lonely remnants of civilisations,
present me with flowers made from plasticine and
faded memories,
to make me feel then defile the beautiful poetry of me.

I miss you sometimes,
those amazing forms of us, the happy us
but you tore us asunder, the psychological warfare
and we're
better left alone in the quiet of this world;

following you through the opaque curtains
through highways and run down houses,
I often want to call you back
and tell you that when I was with you
I was more alone than alone.

Wet and sleepless nights spent mildly aware
with your cold exactitude and my scaffolds of hair,
my ringlets of dreams and intricate as lace wings
adrift in the tendrils of night as I see what dreams
bring;

comfortably numb with my visions of you,
if this world will collapse I will create one a new
and I will sit pretty in this mountain of us
with my ramshackle dreams and my flowers of rust.

Treading into day and night

The terminal velocity of your eyes
are passages of night
trailing needles across my lips
in a soft agony of secret verbs,
my whispers are on your fingertips,
and you are both day and night in perfect unison,
the moon is a poem,
clad in your hair;
I sense she loves us,
motions us to be in both worlds
as you melt into my aching arms,
burning with light
like a silent spectre.

Whisper you're mine,
until the memory of my touch is erased from the
footholds of time
and I have become transient dust,
the afterthought of the universe.

Your Smiles

Your smiles
bleeding into the dormant ghost passages of my eyes
to become a sonnet of morning,
and I have never seen a day like you,
the agony of my changing aura
erupting slowly
into the root-like structures of your phosphorescence
spluttering awake with this new carbon dioxide
and filling with goodness;

the stars will remember us
because our names are etched into the night,
into her cosy purple gloves,
they are alive and shrilly ring
with the soft blankets of amplified insect cries,
and their exoskeleton forms,
have in turn become the landmarks
in the inner most secret maps of my heart.

Truth easily relayed through the wet clichés

Numbers mean things that I don't quite comprehend
as the evening collapses;
I can't forget those words in this brief silence,
the numerology I don't quite get...
and your sweet patience,
they circle around me and make me nervous
as I walk down peeling corridors
with sonnets in my mind
remembering,
them.

You.

Falling into your verbal imagery
as I walk alone
always, always,
alone with your words
walking past dilapidated ruins
of your voice.

I fear that, I'm going to go insane in a wheelchair
staring at the sea
of torn down buildings
as I was always.......
alone,
just like the way I became yours.

Something wicked this way comes

She sent my love to the gallows
with visions masked by musk
with sap stung lips of honey
in the violet equinox of dusk,

and his neck was beautifully decorated
just like it was before,
stained by roses in the twilight
stained with her violence forever more,

but he hung with a new awakening
like a still paradox in the gloam,
kept awake with the hum of my colours
kept awake by his dream of home,

and without sound or expectation
she sent my love to Antarctica
where he grew a shiny new heart
where he blossomed like wine
in the alignment of waking
and never assumed we were apart,

he came back from the glamour of nowhere,
came back with his volatile hands,
he returned with my oceanic turtles
who were devoid of her sharp teeth
and her demands,

I grew clay wings in the sea grass
where the monsters there are kind
and showed my heart to his captor

as he was never far from my mind,

she saw his smile etched in his eyes like granite
back on that cold foreshore
so she crawled back into her empty shell
and bothered us no more.

Your touch, your words

All my poems to you are wet clichés
you tell me you can understand them,
as you whisper words to me under the muffled moon
and they trail down your lips,

down

down

oh god..... down
and onto me
past those sentient rambling,
d i s t a n t
eyes of mine
past the small of my back.

Your touch is a series of actions,
touch –oh... your touch
making sense of my world
through your fingers
plastered on my parchment heart,
like wet paintings
in all my favourite colours.

You could break me.

Breaking can be done
past the wet recesses of my mind
or your numerous, cables of touch
and post-mortem mutilation of my voice
in the flames of your bed.

I explain this endlessly to you
with only my aching body
all through the soft decay of the day
in this torment of night
the night has killed everything else
but god she's alive
in her velvet succession ... god yeah... alive
she's teeming with
with bats, cicadas,
a million insect skeletons
your touch
your words
my shy transfixed, unsophisticated mouth
my soft mess of verbs.

Your eyes meet mine

Your eyes meet mine
because the world has collapsed
leaving in its wake
only just about a million squid tentacles
in the warm radiation of faintly scented pine;

your eyes meet mine
because we awoke after so long
from our sonar visions, being
ever mindful of the cold, deserted caves
of 'their eyes'
with our deep windows
and their iris circling rinds;

your eyes meet mine
dressed in personable attire
because we are so much more than
pure surface, in this wet
disconnection of time;

because I willed you here
past the decomposition of birds,
those dark nefarious pigeons
sweating in every corner
weathering the storms of my mind.

A controlled existence

Stimulate me with unusual scenes, lucid dreams.

Through a controlled existence,
I anti climax
With dried up creative juices,
They're only recalled through blood lust,
A new carnality for membrane and mucus.

I envisioned a beautiful landscape of memories
through muffled sounds and body heat
and solitude within moonlit sheets.

Where my only emotion was wet apathy
and I longed for my soul to be set free.

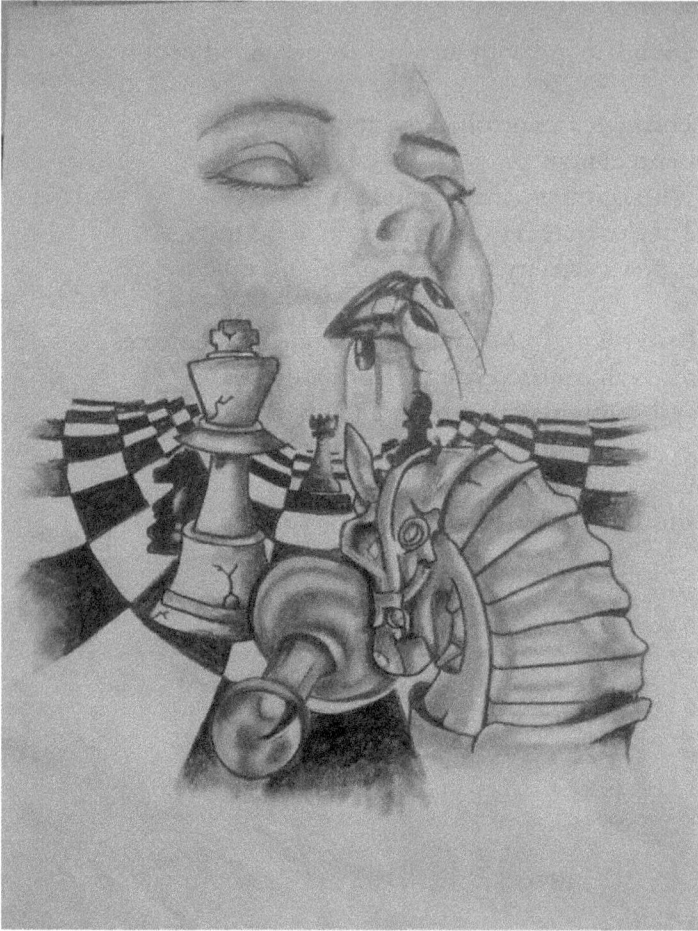

Calling

In tonal harmonies
and long mournful notes
that appeal to the voiceless,
too beautiful to articulate in any lucid terms
I called to you
from beyond the oceans.

You, Oh glorious visionary
architect of my soul.

My heart ached to once again
witness the clairvoyance of you.

Hell

'He' offered me a drink,
it went down easy like delusion
and presented me with whole boxes of tissues,
antibodies
as he promised me the world;

outside I watched on
my whole body was in there
in 'his' cold house
filled with a
silent
ache
for you;

I was born just about this grimy
and my concrete form
was being eaten alive by
the shade
mothballs,
'his' far too natural intentions
and you;

please stamp out the fire in my heart
extinguish the flame
that has been burning since you took my hand
and I trembled with that
whole body
of mine
as my eyes
turned to the sky
in some quasi-religious

resemblance of light;

you long ago removed the rusty signs
that others had left
they'd lain dormant
for so long
in that cold, hard cavity
of my chest
that read 'Hell.'

Come now soft winter and embrace
my longing and discontent;
the brave soldiers have produced lovely images
of a time we remembered collectively,
a microcosm of smells and weak
magnetic signals of sexual magic.

Draining

Too tired
to notice
the slow
draining
of me
and so I
wait
until
my whole reality
bled, red membrane red.

Too slow
to notice
how I
have disappeared
without even a last farewell;
how I am
no longer
still alive
except for the
horrible scent
of you.

The Elephants

In this long summer of us,
you clutch my hand in the wet sunshine
as I lay gently beside you
and whisper only of the elephants,

but you only see my second rate imitations
in obsessed delirium.

I spent all night pouring my soul
into crowded notebooks,
recreating our lost moments of touch,
but you only saw gibberish
and scribbles with biros, pencils and crayons......
and the elephant shaped mess of my world.

Great, big, real, whole, sagging,
floating, moving, busy, grey and brown creatures
are loose in the hospitals, streets,
alley ways, bus stops,
crammed in trains,
restaurants and supermarkets!

I perch among them and try to reach these lithe,
discarnate beings with my long lamenting stares,
my soulful poetry and my magic mantra
that consists of the one word 'elephants,'
I touch your fiercely, warm centre
with a smiling, separated face,
as kaleidoscopic dandelions
brush against the nucleus of my pain,
my eyes graze the cumulus sky

I tell you softly about the shapes of clouds
but I really only see the elephants.

I will go

Your eyes are windows of confused light
bleeding into amber waves of warm liquid moments,
but I will let you go,
as I settle in the boats
that scatter like spots in the floating ephemera
of surreal lights signalling a last goodbye
from the horizon;
I will bid you farewell
as the last leaf falls into the decaying masterpieces
of rustic hued pillows.

We drop hands
and the cool crisp air spells emptiness
in long dead languages
that only the elder trees remember,
and you too will fall from my life;
you will fall like silent prayers from my sullen lips,
tears gathering like swollen bodies
in their agonising release
from the tar dark catacombs
of the spiralling night,
found at the end of hate.

I will leave you there in the emptiness
of singular footsteps
on familiar paths carved from my singular suffering;
I will leave you there and I will find myself;
I will release you like drowning victims
full of leaves and lifelessness
and not look into your soul one last time
I leave you there and find myself

with only my courage
and the knowledge that I forged journeys
with broken wings
and I will accept the winds of fate.

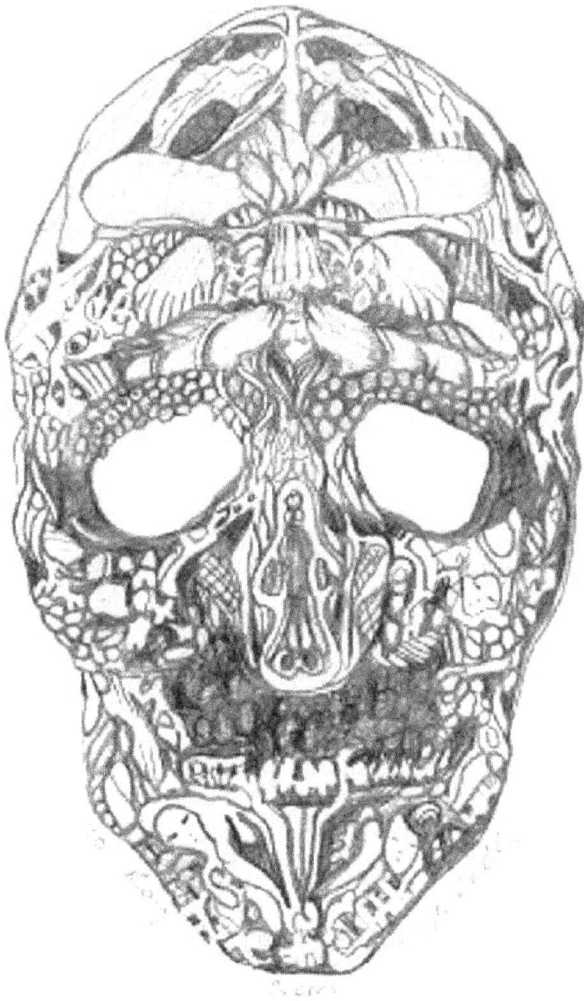

How to host parties or we're all liars anyway

I trip on the darkness,
and on demonic spittle in wet clammy kingdoms,
as giants press
their hands firmly around their mouths beneath the
catacombs of irony and
rent bedroom fortresses,
whilst nebulous curtains block those gods
from entering with their hate dolls,
rubbing their bleary eyes they're forever searching for
rest.

You presented me with flowers plucked from your tears
and called them weeds
under the scrutiny of their madness;
you held my hand and stopped me from falling
into the void
with your quiet concerns.

So I call all weeds flowers
for they are permanently lovely
and help me find my way
when all ghost lamps dim
and I too am lost,
and all poems are left unfinished

Hold me

Your hands
meat hammocks
fleshy knuckles
tubes of moist truth
that relax into my rent form
convex hills,
ridges;
the secret galaxies of my concealed bones bound in
blood,
like horrible pacts.

Hold me a sum of fluids cased in arteries and cells,
my atoms appear as miniature insect skeletons,
these oddly shaped miracles,
a symbiotic mess that bring me life;
I see my internal mechanisms
as abandoned sex crimes
with the evidence of electrical tape, rope, tears,
so many signs of violence
left against freeways to be found by cyclists.

You hold me,
my whole intact body,
alive with goose Braille nightmares read in flesh;
you clutch me like death veils on ancient flesh
flesh that had once known both the endless,
glorious summers stretching into about forever
and the coldness of winter's discontent.

Those cold, dead
almost absent muscles

that had once moved
with the literal motion of pain,
stagger hesitantly into blank tomorrows
like I do now,
silently
in my mind
you hold me without eloquence,
firmly,
how I want you to,
and see
nothing.

Couch fort love

I'll lend you my eyes to curl up in,
my hair to grind against,
my wrists to tangle your fingers in;
offer you this couch as our altar,
your neck is a perfumed bond
that destroys me,
so bound my limbs ten times tonight
tighter than in my tenfold dreams
where your soft growls
meet on my neck, behind my ear
taking
s l o w
l u n g e s
to find secret worlds
unexplored by man,
in our couch fort love;
my lips now moist from my absent years of you,
dripping with your unknown secrets,
your lips stealing my words before I can speak them,
as the T.V blares in the background,
my long fingers bent by the
l o n g e s t of longings,
transfixed against game shows;
if you want to be with me
in this soft torment of night
and continue to whisper
my name,
in laboured sounds,
I will build a tower for us
here on this couch,
under these covers,

and burn your name into
all the doors and soft furnishings,
as you hold me closely
with your beautiful hands
that pulse with miracles.

Enter the dream

Your mind carved up strange images and transported
them to me
seamlessly through your clairvoyance in this long night
absent of
touch.

Whilst I am alone, the air is alive, heavy with prose,
belladonna,
Presque vu frustration.

Endlessly rearranging lucid patterns in deadly
nightscapes,
traversing this new dream,
where my terrible imaginings and I
sit facing in the electrified night,
quickened by sentences both lost and
never spoken;

Imprisoned by perfumed bonds he unties my limbs,
while dark mutterings calluses his lips,
we're both chaffed by monsters in this long cold
kitchen of my soul.

Quivering, this horrible imagination finishes my
soliloquies with dream dust,
whilst veins laden with warm structures fill its breath
with the nausea of catacombs, honeycomb razors on
velveteen
molasses,
as regret stained red, cellular atrophy collapses
into anti-reason

with a smile.

Armed with madness I enter this hot dream to find you,
your waiting arms of chaos the last refuge for my sanity,
while the world
hallucinates second rate miracles around us.

That dark figure
engraved our names
into the soft flesh
of that tree.

Our crimes are carmine coloured
and crimson, like the wet death
of our love.

This haunting place,
reminds me of your
harrowing silence,
our cold words,
used up promises
and unrelenting regrets.

The house of otherness

I tear myself apart in the house of nothing;
the house of boarded up windows and sweet lies
that cling like cobwebs on rigamortis hands,
concrete eyes.

I never invited you in to this hard place of otherness,
where I forget to love you,
where my urgent suffering words lick my pages of
hurried thoughts
outside.

I can forget you in the rain
and run like wolves in the commotion of new spring.

Inside
I'm trapped in this hallway of bleak winter
with the moon heavy on my chest
forcing me out of the safety of darkness,
where you describe the hell I conceive
with barren and pointless smiles
relaying the dark fable of us
iced with misunderstanding
and Chinese whispers of absconded hearts.

Pssssssssssst Hey.....

"Hey"
my words fall gently like gossamer webs
and penetrate like blood
under unvarnished nails
on footpaths
or peeling wallpaper
warm
like the dying embers of sleep
with your name lying limp and boneless on their lips
in the coldest moments of the still night;
years have decorated your eyes in this
autumn of us,
where tracks are carved from miseries that time forgot
and dreams take their last breath,
my sharp instruments
run wild like brumbies in the hard brush
heaving as they rise
galloping, jumping and landing deep in liquid cavities
in whole rivers
and I whisper
like honey on razors
without control of reigns.

"Hey"
the word echoing in the still air
like the dying sounds of the conductor
as the soul train
finally departs.

"Hey"
my mouth curled in cruel

116

paralysis with the word still glued
in the secret crevices of my lips
its lyrical poison
making me crazed,
and you thought that when the demons claimed their
final kiss
it would be like all swift things, beautiful
and so you dreamt of brumbies
that are so unlike my long frenzied descent into this
cold desert of madness
that slowly tapers through the cracks in my smile
and spills down my face in tears.

Restraint

The noise of my heart
burning in common terms,
ripping your poetry from out of my ears,
like the remnants of dreams;
dull grey particles,
soul-shaped wonders,
staggering into the nearest decay
of my lips;
words stripped of form,
swaying with unuttered contempt.

I just may never come back from this dream,
and the smell of my heart strings
permeate my skin,
like the cigarette stained felt of your hands,
I want to smell like the furnace of secret petals,
a landscape of colour as I burn
in silence;
come closer before I melt into consciousness,
before I'm moulded into a template
of twisted veins and skeletal, sculptural flecks
of molten temperance.

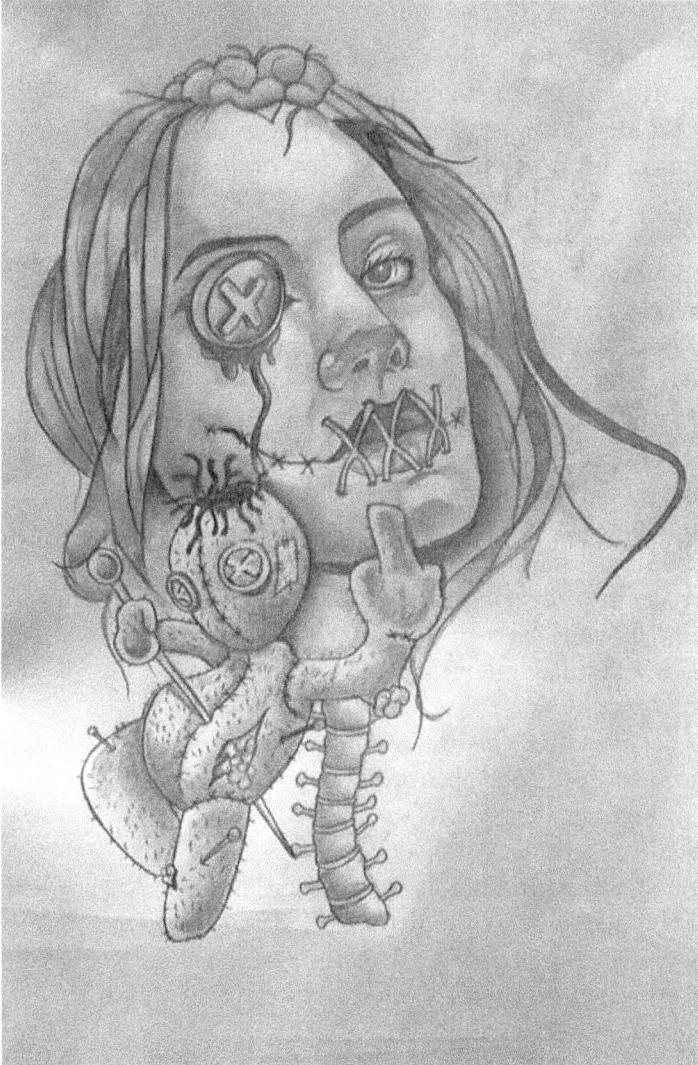

All windows are doors

I was dreaming universes of your touch
with crazy abstract meanderings
peeking through nights of tall spirits
raising my eyelashes, hoping they'd notice me
(all the invisible worlds)
my wine drenched head spins
in circus winds,
so clutch my cold fingers and whisper to me of
forest nymphs and madness in this cold air.

I swallowed the warm honey drenched scents
of dark possibilities,
my pocket watch hands
ticking slowly, coating my relaxed mouth
while the delicious hum of the clouds
melts into my eyes,
like the whole cosmos
is my familiar.

I decided that I wanted my insides
to be a Daliesque appropriation
in the dark shades of your soul;
a surreal universe pulled me apart
from within and made me art personified;
I was a kaleidoscope of ancient gods,
an amalgamation of your dark presence,
a culmination of our smiles,
a pan dimensional night,
and all windows were doors
to wondrous gardens.

Clawing with my scales and nails and flesh-coloured
asphyxiation,
you shake doubt from your mouth as you let horrible
sentences fall freely
down your lips like sludge.

I bought you a gift, wrapped it in your favourite lies
and called it all the promises you outgrew.

Charlie don't dance or private winters of your smile

The veil of reality
blinding my eyes like a million tiny needles
that hunger for your soft skin;
under the cavities of sun drenched confused light
the nerves of my tireless planets
are cloudy in my skull
like freshly extinguished furnaces,
smoke fuels my tragic electrons
that constantly glean your touch.

Bit, by bit, by bit.

But you feel your veins gradually turning to magnets,
rare cancers opening like zippers,
on your lips
blooming with the
roses and
kisses,
and with those pursed pockets of
black winters,
you fall from my life.

Shuffling my fingernails against the soft tangent of
space
where you once stood,
the magic lights echoing incoherently
are the only proof
you were once here
with me.

Bitter were the tears I shed
that danced about eyelids of lead,
as my imagination fed
with no distinction between alive or dead.

Spaces within spaces

My heart played sad comedies
for cold blooded lizards to laugh at,
their carrion breath washed over me
and all my nights were spent looking at
empty spaces
within spaces.

The lady boys don't fancy me
and Kurt Cobain was never a poet
and all sharp objects spoke to me far more than his
words.

The cascading breath of night washed over me with her
deadpan gaze,
like I was her illegitimate step-daughter
she rented spaces in my head,
spaces
within spaces
and whispered to me of death
with her long drawn out drawl
in a cold and haunting voice that spoke only of its
warmth,
its painlessness.

I woke up in an old truck
I couldn't follow my thoughts.

Kurt Cobain watched on, he was a wet genius,
his words trailed down his disembodied mane,
as my lips gradually closed in atrophy;
until only my mind remained active,

his words spoke to me of a deep golden nothingness
more than
the amber wings of light that fell onto my cold cheeks
and made my voice silent.

He showed me the face of god in every flower,
but god was drunk and laughing at my tears again
whilst I was strung out on neon images of his
unempathetic face
in horror
with the error of his engines in my ears.

Ha HA ha HA
till my eyes are a happy river of time,
until my thoughts escape me,
until I'm an empty Venus, a sexless colossus,
a broken sentence,
Kurt Cobain was a......

I awake in the cold reality of reason
but my thoughts are lost in some dry universe,
with only the persistence of memory.

Losers

Dark and doorless eyes had stolen our confidence,
Father Time too, chipped away at it constantly,
so we,
these silent monuments turned inward on our axis
and lay witness to our gradual disappearing
on corners with no edges
and M. C. Escher became our poetry.

But these invisible hands, bloodless miracles
have now been lifted from the inner sanctum of our
shoulders
and now we have absently followed footsteps left from
transient nobodies,
like ants up walls into the translucent veins of the skies
and listened to owls that no longer refused to
acknowledge us
and become the exquisite losers of our own destinies.

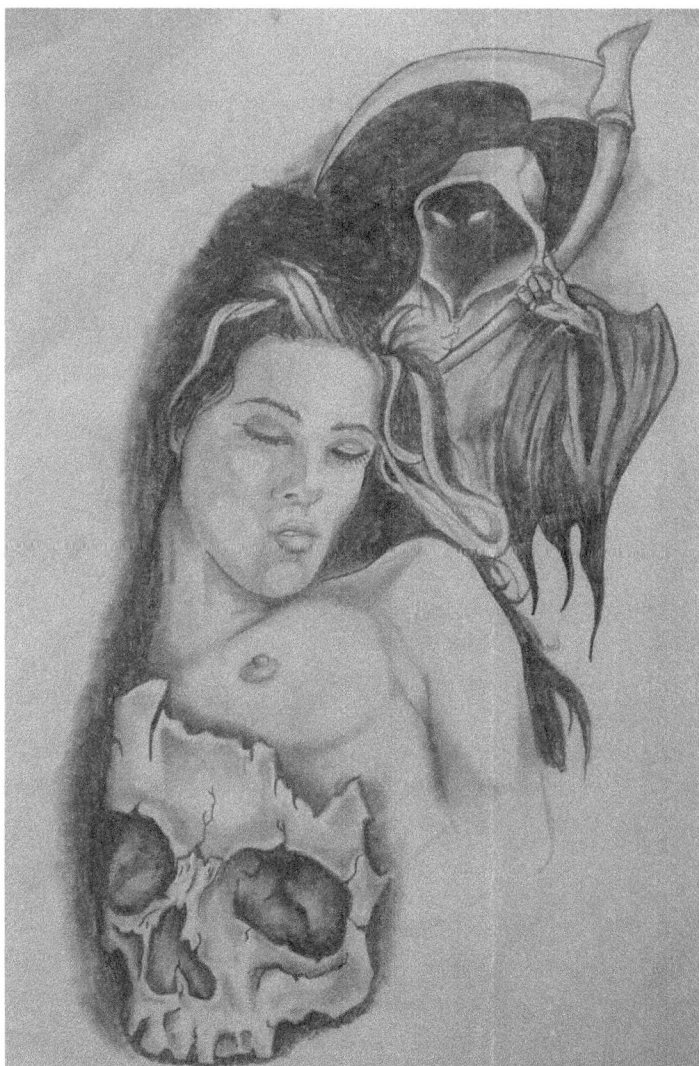

For Roy

He had clouds burnt into his eyes,
his cigarette smoke tracing ladders to a beautiful
elsewhere,
and books upon books etched into his palms that spelt
'life.'

He made me want to spit out my dreams
in soliloquies to bag ladies
and memorise Pablo Neruda
and surrender myself completely
to the felt of the skies,
as the nerves of the wind blew softly around us in quiet
dissidence.

He trailed magic strokes of invisible ink
into the crowded supermarkets and streets
and spoke of art like carnivals;
he made me understand that I could fall completely
apart
and put myself together again,
as oceans or poetry—that I was more than just the
sinking boats in my heart.

Words fell from his lips like singular miracles
and I felt like I could rewrite history—all history,
and he brushed them off
like they weren't the grimy masterpieces on the
bathroom walls of my soul...
and drew darker shades with his pencils
that echoed a truth far beyond
reason.

Distant Universes

Testing the fixtures of reality,
heirloom varieties of us in the greying day,
huddled in the caress of the softly lit
radiation of distant universes,
with the perfect formation of words on your lips.

Forget that I am unsophisticated
and I'll forget all the golden dawns
that have exploded under your eyelids,
that have given rise to my aching arms.

But let me keep the stars
and the tapestry of memories
woven into the deepest cavities of my heart.

Your lips

Your lips are sonnets for reason,
moist metaphors for light;
they speak to me of honey,
they make my voice quiet.

There's an echo of movement
in the broken symmetry of my eyes;
I'm rehashing your dark script
once again in my mind,
but you're a reason to write again,
when novelists bear their wings
your mouth keeps dripping honey
and in its sweetness it stings;
I'm hunching my shoulders,
I can't show you my art,
and I'm crouched on the edge
barricading my heart.

The inexplicable beauty of falling

I fell into a star
and confessed
with my three hearts
how beautiful I found the shapes
and lines around your eyes;
I drank your synergy
like a glassy eyed miracle
and gleaned your secret knowledge
of the rent universe
through the fabric of your hands.

All the nerves of the skies
have no walls any more,
just a soft intimacy
from which I can fall;
they're raw and removed from
the rusted pages of heartache
that stick like tar to trees
in the cool collapse of the night.

My eyes are held open with
visions and all consuming
spectres of sound
dripping from the pieces
of broken, fragmented highways
of the auto erotic, audio
of your lips;
I was grinning like
wolves in the sonnet of night
feeling cocooned by the covers
coupled with your collapsing weight on mine.

This rotting

He moves like a boneless angel
on his rattled thighs;
He's sexless,
his mouth dripping with
carrion cries.

He's phosphorous,
He's poisonous,
and the only void in the night
is his rent crystalline eyes.

But there's an algorithm for everything,
even for the lament of this soft light;
I'm consuming his poison,
I'm confused at best,
He's glowing and green
half asleep on my chest;
my heart is a frozen river
of unfathomable depth,
deep and disturbed
by coldness and death.

His heart like a rose
in the end of May days,
with a lost echo of life
mostly withered away.

And we clutch at each other
in a sexless daze,
through the dying heat of the night,
his grasp the tightest macabre,

132

tarnished like mirrors,
consuming what's left
of my ashen gaze
in his falling breath.

The skeleton of the bead frame,
a euphemism for us
in this corpse of mattered sheets,
these cold springs of a rust.

Where the worms start to rampage
and the words start to leave me
where I begin to feel this rotting
that will someday set us free.

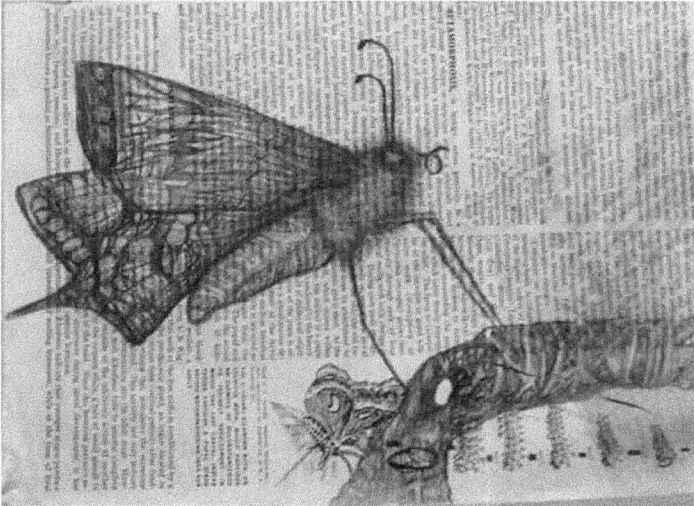

Time don't dance like I do

There are long roads approaching
at break neck speeds,
white knuckles and the spittle of time
spreading out cold despondent over there.

S l o w i n g down,
speeding up
Sp lut ter ing!!!
dying on me man!

In her bed of sea grass and vomit,
and in the horror of the real
whole sagging, grey gestures
grapple with the nightmare of youth
that defecates in every corner.

Ignore that horror show of us aching in places
where we as younger cats played,
sliding razors in deep rivers of crimson
across the gaunt, forever changing
faces of time and melancholia in her madness.

And I kiss away your tears,
where winter encountered your cheeks
with my sincere heart.

Haiku

Death throes of your lips,
reverberating soft sounds.
Those old magic words.

Completely destroyed,
your eyes in the Autumn dusk
make me dream of dawn.

How pleasing your touch
here, pressed into the warm earth
worms dig silently.

Your voice of honey,
magic structures of your breath,
I have seen nothing.

I think I can really see you
and I want you to really see me too.

You see ...where those beautiful symmetrical machines viewed
an asphalt jungle of buildings
I saw visions of quantum worlds between the cracks,
and this is the version of my world that I want you to
see too.

And
when you're pulled under the covers of absolute night
or buried in arid landscapes by hands who have
neglected you;
when your broken heart is a tomb,
forgotten in the nonsense of moon sand in some
desolate universe;

when you feel betrayal in the wind but your lungs hurt
from the suffering of
a silent breeze that only you feel;

when all you can say as you desperately cling to dry
banks,
holding back rivers of tears
through gritted teeth,
fighting back adjectives,
and other subtle nuances.

Is...

'Fuck This Shit' FuCK, fuckity fuck
fuck...............................

You need no words.

They fail every time to express your galaxy
of
....
....

And we'll both fight to be eloquent.

In your adversity,
 'Bats fly together'
'worms feed together'
'lemmings die together.'
And anyway I'm no angel.........
And sometimes I string together uninteresting words to
form non-lucid structures.

And as you spit my hair from out of your mouth,
you clean the grime from out of my wasted heart.

Find my halo amongst the forgotten, broken, Christmas
ornaments;
Roll back the lid of my forgotten tomb and untie me.

Lost

Some secrets become lost,
some epics are written
on receipts on the train
or housed in the rotting
warehouse of your brain.

If love is a secret,
let all secrets remain;
I won't speak about it,
not to demons of the deep,
not through foghorns or whiskey
or the promises I can't keep.

And anyway they're all lost.

We're all lost,
transfixed on the brine
or salvaged by cliffs
who refuse to speak rhyme,
and if somehow they escape
from your mouth to mine,
translation can't mimic
what the tongue tries to find;
that cursive elusive, ovation
some turn to vapour,
even through the frost,
or though the mess swords sometimes make
or somehow tip-toe into paper,
and they too become lost,
and anyway those secrets don't escape
the embers of your eyes;

they're transfixed by the light
and your lyrics on paper
are exposed to the night,
are always dodging the candles
that half lit up the bay,
as Davy Jones whispered

'I just got lost on the way'

Wrecks

I bent my ears closer to forever to catch the words
whispered though lips as dry as moon sand
in secret places
but those words are old
about as aged as stagnant dams
holding rotten figures with long forgotten names
they speak only of our pasts
and have nothing more to say.

So I trailed my hands blindly across the skin of my
exposed legs,
carefully spelling out your name in the Braille of my
goose bumps,
I read there in that absent touch
about how you too have been broken.

As I curled my arms around myself feeling my own
damaged touch
that's barely warm,
I feel that we have become closer
as I sit alone in this empty house
where no one can touch me
in cruelty or in sympathy.

I have been travelling in my thoughts,
clutching broken pieces of you.

You held on to my own shattered pieces,
as we tried to mend one another with promises
or handles stolen from objects that had known no
different

140

when we had fooled them with our smiles,
and those we tricked with glue
never knew of the stained wool we had stuffed into
our wounds or the moths we had sewed into our hearts
to make beat again.

In taking your hand you have led me to see
how two wrecks leaning together at this angle are no
longer tragic,
instead they become stronger
and far more beautiful.

Cicadas and smiles

Carved in bone your velvet voice collapses into smiles,
like explosions of honey
into the cigarette stale air I cling onto,
hanging down the damp recorded dreams of your eyes.

Those musty, transfixed holograms distort pain into
soft dunes,
new opportunities,
echoing shadows and exotic lands far off into the
distance;
deep pools, soft visuals ,
those dormant windows lead outwards
into endless hazel rivers that touch the sky.

Tinted by the exile of vanished whispers,
my dying breath touches your skin,
dances on the windows
competes with a million cicadas longing for petals,
all moaning, all lusting in the fractured dusk, their cries
burning into my
ears.

In this warm collapse of day,
this liquid evening of burnt umber
and a feint rhythm of a clock's minute hand
replaying in déjà vu dreamscapes,
there's just us in this empty room,
us and my dislocation, it's a series of endless
stupid questioning
in the dark romance of my soul
and collapsing tides of you.

142

You.

As warm dark, insect chords
fuse into the audio of strange internal landscapes in
layers,
my vacant touch lingers in the empty corners of your
magic wrinkles;
you're wearing those same clothes that you love
as you walk around the room
into the ghosts of summer nights,
into the late rainfall of endless exoskeletal forms,
minute insect skeletons,
you with that damn impossibly beautiful smile,
pure like your drug of choice,
bruised into the dark, black, blood tides of your lips,
untainted by the twisted, squid ink, bleakness of my
voice,
unfading like the impossible outlines of this room's
bones,
and fractals of light,
as you pour me another
and smile.

Walls

Sleepily
the peat moss remembers
and delights in the nights
decorated by shadows
from places kittens mew
in wait with padded paws.

A slow decent once winter went
with cellophane days
in visions bent,
the former world
that passed away
curls inwards,
snarling.

Sandwiches,
I make them
in my nucleus webs,
where tree frogs
are silent.

The house
flickers,
then plays dead games,
as bleach
kills microcosms,
as I stare at spots on walls.

Salty smiles

He holds my face with his gnarled beauty
resting like feather ghosts on my liquid streams of
consciousness,
while I clutch spoons and saucepans
and mix tears with sauce
in the half light.

Stroking my hair,
music plays,
his touch is warm,
dinner cooks,
neurons fire,
a soft smile burns into the wrinkles around my mouth
where I encounter him,

as my eyelashes kiss his hands.

Ardent fires,
cradle the need in my soul
in the quiet of your face.

Will you.......

bury my radiant smile in all your
oblong boxes where you hide.....
all your secret things?

and...... relax your body into mine
for one last final kiss...
like you've done
to the sun?

(if I stared too long into tomorrow)
it is because I panicked I'd forget,
you'd forget
and I lanced your touch like lace winged figures
startled
...ghosts
ceramic eyes
fading like your smiles
dancing slowly like...
the lost words on your lips.......
horrible truth,

like how well you know
the cold furnace of my dark heart
I'd left to rot
with all the mistakes
I've made
rust
like
lids
left
on

paint cans
and capture my essence in quick,
violent truths
b****
c*****
if my essence is worth words to you
and let those words
die on your tongue
we were not meant to linger.

I can't write...my words just can't convey my quivering
mess of incoherence... I can only focus on a dream of us, and my brain waves
dissolve into empty rays of graphite toned, grey waves of endlessness on paper,
flushed with crumpled words, caressing one another in an edifice of lined,
washed-out, pencil carved, heavy handed scraps of poetry, from the multiplying
rivers, sand and sewers of my mind.... I can only tell you that my thoughts are
scattered like rent, light piercing the dark room of my soul in lifelines of ink madness
.... fuck.. there is no eliminating, no elevating, no alleviating, and no escaping
from this nocturnal realm...these ....imaginings....

.I'll tell you of my dream! A voice cleaved
the world in two like a heavy sexual current.. my man (whom I love) stands inside
the void, he has a strong jaw like a wolf... a black lipped beast, eyes, yellow like
royalty, eyelashes sweeping me down blood-lust streams of his chiselled cheeks
of stone into his lips of heavy scented tobacco tomorrow and his heart is big and
bright and golden like stars entering the atmosphere burning into the cold engine of empty,
meaningless night in a forest of veins and jewels and his wings
are magnificent globes of night foretelling the future.

He has a forest of fingers
touching every hair on my soft pheromone head in
circular madness. This is why
my tongue has gone mute beside him and my words
have become as meaningless as this passage...
mumble...
my hands are thick bricks of anti-progress
and I can't write...

Sunshine

I wonder how many times those lips have
performed miracles under the cloak of day,
how many of your words like bullets
have perforated the hardened shell,

of her, or
of her,

and made the love pour out,
without shame,
in this rain of sunshine
that I assign
anthropomorphic qualities to.

Your eyes are camouflaged by their need,
pretending to be dead like children in school yards,
those private snuff movies in your wet skull
are changing her forever,
like the patterns of the sand and sea and sky,
resolute and silent,
like the film noir journey
back to your man lair,

and she knows
she shouldn't be there,
but the world has gone away,
blank and forgotten,
the memories erased,
like sleeping babes in hot cars,
like upturned bikes,
in a mess of cries,

like a mother's long, dead warning,

and one day soon you'll see her
through
glass,
or mirrors.

Forgotten,
like a sex crime out on the highway,
like our used up lines,
she's still searching for something inexplicable,
outside in the hot sunshine.

Cats purr too

Under moonlit drenched paths,
with confused liquid cavities,
invisible circuses of pain,
carnivals in my dark eyes,
ghosts on my lips,
pulling automatic strings,
making odd sounds come out,
I mouth those words
'cats purr too.'

Bugs fly together and fall,
maggots are born,
fat and happy
in my brain,
for I have so many rotten thoughts
and they're hungry for filth,
devils are stuck under my fingers,
guiding blunt objects,
shadows are silent spectres,
making my face bleed in all kinds
of boats of kinetic sadness,
and cats purr too.

Those beasts knew me under my dress
and I spoke all kinds of brave words to them
in blue lies with all strange, bug stung
tongues,

and you never believed me,
and their cold words stick in my throat,
and I just may never come back from this dream

and cats purr too.

I sink like bodies in rust filled pools,
my knees bent like twisted limbs in odd angles,
my eyes tombs for honey, and light,
and burst with full moons of sound and sight,
I'm filled with about a million holes,
where the love pours out,
a red hypothesis of rent twilight,
and cats purr too.

A cold night shared freely

He spat sonnets from dreams
in the smoke filled aura of night
and his lips skip, too light for spells
that he never speaks
delicately.

This evening is lit by torn down towers,
but he is a building, built up by beauty
in the hard corners,
just begging to be destroyed.

Posture as serene as the waves,
eyes as telling as pictures,
and he hates the way
I want to be played,
like a light filled ruse
of iris, of coral,
circling wet circumstances,
painterly echoing the tragedy of me,
speaking in old tongues,
corrupted with Blake type imagery,
as I speak with my hands without reasoning
of what ignites me.

Dew,
magic scents,
promises,
long dead gods.

As his smoke joins my lips in the cold air,
we're connected by a silent trail

of grey somewhere,
forcing its way into my own lungs,
destroying me,
ever so slowly,
just like he does.

Beautiful doesn't even come close to describing him,
caught on the poems of his face,
in this ugly longing,
I write words that mean nothing,
to placate my hands,
redirect my suffering.

He speaks in cursive

He is a beautiful somewhere,
his eyes echo a past
violence
in descriptive cursive,
mirrors of mine
collapse.

His warmth conductive,
silk, delicate
movement in shadows,
moisture of past druids,
insomnia.

He drew new horizons
into all my empty
tomorrows
with his flecks of
pain,
life,
decorative brilliance,
I just knew he would
save me.

His words are miracles
that pulsate into the gloam,
as we speak in softness,
pliable waves
of diffused light
and dust.

The wreckage of the world

escapes my notice,
as we walk in different worlds,
as my heart opens like
a pill-box miracle.

Day 7

Purple gloves of night blanket the landscape in
gossamer webs,
as minute freckles kiss her pearl drop tears with tender
nuances.

Invisible cicadas wave goodbye
to the sun drenched trees resting on the horizon;
the last burnt sienna tree tops disappear leaving feint
lipstick stained memories.

She weaves strange, orange scented forget-me-nots
into the garlands of her long ebony tresses
like collisions of dusk and whole golden summers.

Moonlit ponds catch her hazel eyes
like explosions of fireworks;
minute bonfires blazing over fresh dew soaked leaves.

She moves like a sonnet:
like drifting dandelions:
like the secrets of my wasted heart.

Her voice an endless series of velvet tides
washing over tired fins,
as silver,
moonlit orbs caress drifting wreckage
to the faint hum of her lips
as she starts her journey home.

the neon ghosts of us wander
while the warm, wet gardens of us
rest in the still daze of the shade flowers

The lights of your eyes bore into mine,
like the web of Indra our infinite galaxies
shine forever in interconnectedness,

Let's lie here in the nape of morning,
our billowy silhouettes stretching
in the warm, organic, spring...
forever... in the measureless,
wonderment of liquidity,

our hungry ghosts procure beautiful,
rainbows of joy luck
in the pandemonium night,
while our effortless gardens show signs of strange
magic
in the soft laughter of morning,

lovely, resolute, organic, us,
we sway with treasures of touch
and smiles of symphonic genius,

our leaves of clairvoyance
vibrate in several playrooms of existence
as our ghosts lean anxiously out windows.

Surely I've known you,
the kinetic sway of you,
felt your form echo mine
in the soft darkness.

sensed your touch
fornicate on the taunt of my flesh
with a long, languished longing,

surely on lonely nights
I have felt your absence
pined for you
as my fingers traced the contours of your face
in invisible squid ink,
on the blank canvass of my being

I picture us in old burnt out cars
with me still trying to touch the cold,
dark furnace of you....
your unseen ink blots
still playing out the simulacrum of our forms
in arcs of wanton magic
on the walls of the hospitals,
supermarkets and laneways of my soul ...

I feel that our clairvoyance was a clear,
hot soup-like substance
that clung to my long, tortured form
in a palpable mess of magnetic south.
and now I can only view you remotely,
the pages of concern on my brow
the universe of regret in your heart.

Day 4

The owl and the butterfly
met in the midst of a beautiful
autumn breeze glow.

The planets aligned
and the signs in the grove
had foretold that their friendship would grow.

The owl hypnotized
by the butterfly's patterns of eyes
begged the insect to stay in his nest,
but the butterfly cried
'we're too different inside,
you have a heart,
while I'm segmented parts,
I'm sorry I can't be your guest.'

So the owl answered back
slow,
in his best voice meek and low,
that
'here we will be safe together'
(but his meaning was grim).

And the owl looked so mild,
so wise and old,
(and he lied)
what he really meant was
they'd be together inside him.

The butterfly cried,

unaware of his lies,
as the owl cradled her close by his side,
and they flew up to the dizzying heights
to the crest of the tree,
to the nest,
and there he took her inside.

She saw all the feathers in the loft,
he showed her his bed,
it was unbelievably soft,
and he promptly bit off her head.

ABOUT THE AUTHOR

Michelle Brown has always had a compulsion to create and has been drawing and writing poetry from a young age, she's attracted not only to the mysterious and the unknown but also to the misfits, troubadours and outcasts of the world, having always felt on the fringe of society herself.

She has a degree in Art History, decorates cakes and is an assistant art educator, her art has been displayed in various exhibitions and venues.

She lives with her partner in crime Roy Austin and his children. Roy is a tattoo artist living in Brisbane Australia.

Michelle Brown's work can also be seen at

https://www.facebook.com/GothicAndEroticPoetry?fref=ts

Roy Austin's work can be seen at

https://www.facebook.com/SinInkTattoo?fref=ts

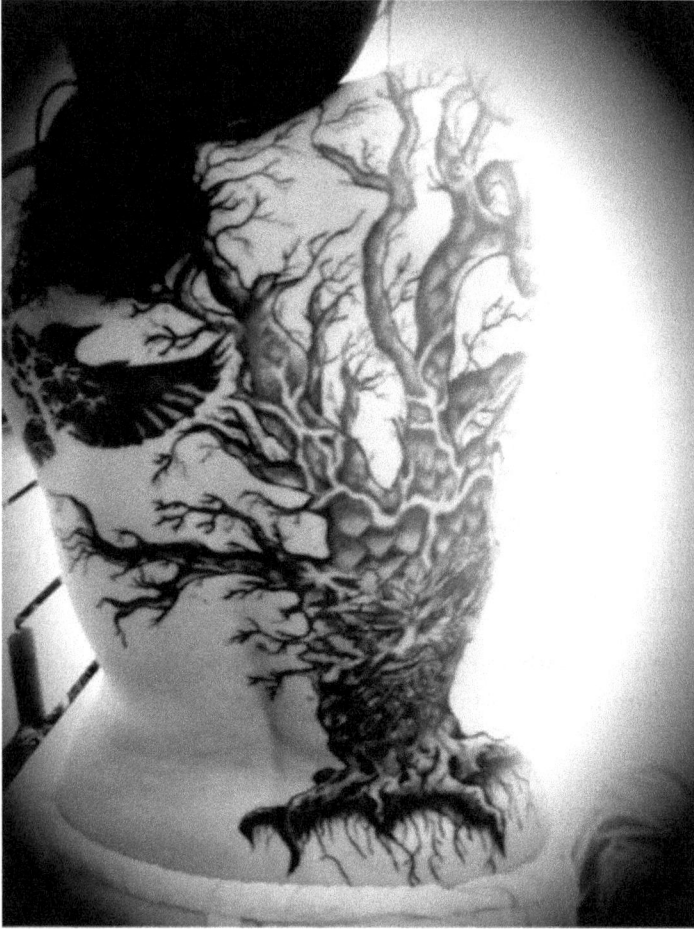

www.ingramcontent.com/pod-product-compliance
Lightning Source LLC
Chambersburg PA
CBHW060014050426
42448CB00012B/2748